TUSKEGEE LOVE LETTERS
By Kim Russell

Red Tails - Tuskegee Airman and family

3395 S. Jones #206
Las Vegas, NV 89146
(702) 248-1232
kimrussell@earthlink.net

CAST:

BERNARD	African-American pilot, writer, comedian, age 23
LUANA	Bernard's wife, African American actress, age 21 (pronounced Lu Ah na)
KIM	Daughter of Luana & Bernard, any age

THE TIME: Story moves from the present back to 1942 and returns to the present

STAGING:

When performed as a static reader's theater presentation the stage should have two chairs side-by-side or at a table. These are for Luana and Bernard with Kim set apart at a podium.

When performed with entrances and exits, each actor should have separate table and chair.

Lighting changes signal changes in days, weeks, years, temperatures and more.

While the early letters are limited to Luana, she should be reacting to and toying with the unseen Bernard.

Letters are written to Mom who is Luana's Mother.

With sincere thanks to Linda Knighten for first discovering these treasures and to Firouzeh Forouzmand and the Las Vegas Clark County Library District for allowing the play to have life.

Dear Reader,

This manuscript contains letters intended to be read aloud. Think of it as an old-fashioned radio play. You-- the listener, sit intently hearing the words with closed eyes, whilst professional actors breathe life into the words on the page. Now imagine a readers theater play – that's where actors sit at a table and become the characters, but they never move from their chairs.

They read. They interpret. They are the characters.

You listen. You imagine. You dream you are the characters.

Approach this reading in a similar fashion - perhaps you read each letter aloud.

To insure clarity, I begin each letter with the name of the author – and if you are reading it like a play, I included a few stage directions.

I hope you enjoy. I hope you are inspired. I hope you find your family treasures, just as I did. Kim Russell

Newlyweds – James Bernard and Luana Knighten
1942

LIGHTS UP ON KIM AND REMAIN FOCUSED UNTIL THE
START OF THE FINAL LETTER

KIM

Before I was born my mother and father shared the events of their lives through letters. Separated by war and duty, they wrote about their joys, their dreams and their individual struggles. Thankfully each preserved their letters, - preserving the V-mails, the handwritten notes, the uneven typed single-spaced pages and postcards. This collection of letters is a glimpse of their lives between the years of 1942 and 1956.

My father was a pilot with the all-Negro Tuskegee Airmen; My mother a steno-typist, and dreamer. For the Tuskegee men and women this was an opportunity to challenge the racial inequalities, the racial stereotypes and the monstrous segregation prevailing throughout the United States; this was a chance to prove Black men capable; to prove Black men can fly. With the advent of World War II, political pressure was exerted to include Negro Americans in the military. The Army Air Corps accepted the challenge, and Tuskegee Institute, founded by Booker T. Washington, in the heart of deeply segregated south, was selected to be the primary flight training site. As a result, the United States Army Air Corps activated the 99th Pursuit Fighter Squadron in March 1941. My Dad was one of the first 15 pilots to complete the program.

These letters are my parent's legacy. They tell about a difficult but wondrous journey filled with obstacles and opportunities for my mother and father. These letters remind us all young Americans begin their lives with dreams.

America is engaged in war. In this first letter my father is in New York state awaiting orders to fly to overseas – destination unknown. He writes the following letter to his mother-in-law:

LIGHTS UP ON BERNARD

BERNARD

My Dear Mom:

I sincerely hope this letter finds you well. I feel badly not having written after taking your daughter away. Whenever you wrote to Luana, she would promptly give me all of its contents, even though I'd be trying desperately to listen to the radio. Now I'm at a loss since she isn't with me to tell me the dirt from Wichita.

I do hope you can read this writing. Your daughter decided to marry me rather than to try and read my letters.

I am in upper New York State and except for California, it is the best place in the United States to live. The land is so nice and the people here don't remind you, you're colored. I'm almost certain that by the time this letter reaches you I will be aboard some ship, headed for I don't know where. I have been trying to rest so in case I have to swim, I'll have all my strength.

Whenever you see your daughter next, she'll have lots of lies to tell about things I said, but don't believe a word of it – all of the fellows here have met some beautiful girl in New York and they are trying to figure some way to get out of going overseas. We all know

how impossible that is. You must write your daughter
as regular as possible, for she throws a real fit when
you don't. I can always tame her down, but now that
I've gone, she might tear little Tuskegee apart.
Best of luck to you.

Sincerely yours, Bernard

KIM

*That's my Dad.   In later years he would be a televised
comedian, an air traffic controller, publish a magazine,
and...well, I'm getting ahead of the story. He and my
mother were married in November 1942 and Luana
experienced a BIG shock moving from St. Louis to
Alabama. At age 21 she was about to experience the
unexpected. Here is a letter from her to her mother, from
Tuskegee, Alabama.*

LIGHTS UP ON LUANA

LUANA

Hi Mummy,

I haven't heard from you in so long I am worried about
you. Are you all right? I am ok as is Bernard. Why
haven't you written me? Surely you received my letter
I wrote you about a week or so ago. I have been so
busy I would have written again but I was so sure that
every day I would hear from you. You know, I told you
in my last letter I was working. I like my job very much.
I don't know whether I will be able to go to work
tomorrow or not. We have had four days of continuous
rain and the bridge is about to be washed away. It has
stopped raining now but it looks like it might start
raining again. If it does we probably won't be able to

get to the field. The buses have stop running. The highway to Montgomery has been washed away.

Well Sis[1] has been here a week now. I got her a job. She starts work tomorrow at the base as a steno – just like I am. I'll tell you about it but keep it to yourself. There is a colored fellow here who has to do with all the hiring of civilians here. As luck would have it, I didn't have to go under him since they came to me and asked if I would work since I wasn't doing anything and I could do clerical work. So I was hired by a white captain. Well I sent Sis to the colored man and being a nigger he says unless she went out with him, she couldn't have the job. She was sick so I told her I would get her a job and then I was going to see him and give him a piece of my mind. And that is just what I did. I didn't tell my boss the real reason I brought her to him, but I told him I would rather she see him, instead of the colored man. He cussed me out saying what did I want him to do, hire my whole G-d--- family! He is a southern cracker but I like him. He cusses all the time. He called up the man and told him where to put her, and to fill out her papers without a civil service test, but to give her a civil service rating, and to give her a damn good one at that. He really jumped then and afterwards I went to turn in my physical exam papers and gave him a sweet sarcastic smile and asked him if he liked his job very much. He looked at me like he was scared to death. He has done so many girls that way and gotten away with it. So many of the people know about it now, but everyone hates to do anything about it, because as sure as he is reported, he will be put, out and a white man put in his place.

---

[1] Nickname for Bernard's younger sister, Allene

This Tuskegee is the dirtiest place in the country. You have taught me that everything in the world was nice and clean, or at least being around you, you have made things seem so, and it really hurts to find out that life isn't really like that. It is between Bernard and me because we make it so. But outside it isn't really like that. I thought people who did things well -- I really don't know how to say it. I mean only people who lived in slums and had no education and knew nothing about morals only did things like going out with lots of men, and drinking and all the lowest things but here, there are people with a string of degrees and money and all the things that go with it and they live like heathens. Gee I hope I will make half the wife and mother that you are. Mrs. Washington teases and baby's me because I'm always saying mother does this, this way or that way. I have become conscious of how much I do talk about you now. (Ha-ha) I don't care, I idolize you and I don't care who knows it. If I'm down here when you get your vacation I want you to visit me. Mrs. Washington is dying to meet you. She is very sweet and pretty. She has beautiful long white hair and a very young face. Nettie, her daughter has really red hair. Nettie's baby is five months old now and she cut two teeth yesterday. We are all so proud of her we call her our child. I think I told you Nettie's husband, Frederick Douglass[2] the 3rd, committed suicide last summer. You probably read about it in the

---

[2] Frederick Douglass III, was great grandson of abolitionist Frederick Douglass and married Nettie Washington, great, grand-daughter of educator Booker T Washington.
Douglass III committed suicide April 10, 1942. Their daughter Nettie Washington Douglass, known as Honey or Nettie III, was born in October.
http://www.ajc.com/news/content/metro/stories/2008/06/26/nettie_dougl ass_washington.html

papers. Anyway the baby is a doll. She laughs all the time and I don't think I have heard her cry but once since I have been here. She is a remarkable baby.

Well I'm getting sleepy now so I will close. Please write soon, it makes me feel very bad when I don't hear from you often. I love you.

Love to all. Lu

KIM

The newlyweds were married in November, enjoyed marital bliss in the winter, but find the spring month of April not as kind. From the office of the Quartermaster, Tuskegee Army Flying School, Tuskegee, Alabama. Written just before members of the 99th left Tuskegee:

LUANA

Hi Mom,

Again I'm at work writing you. I don't feel so sporty today. I have a cold and on top of that I'm worried about Bernard. Well I'm not exactly worried but a little blue. I certainly hate to see him go. Last night was his last night home.

Of course I don't let Bernard know I am sad. He is quite confident about going, so that makes me feel better. He says if any man comes out of the 99th alive you can bet your life he will be among them. He told me if I received a letter from the government, saying he was missing or a prisoner of war for me not to worry. He had probably landed in some neutral country and would be having a ball.   Bernard is really a nut. I'm hoping he will only have six months of combat and then come back here for the duration. This may happen as it does for so many of the white fellows.

Saturday, when I get paid, I'm going to send you some money and will you get me a pair of comfy shoes and some good shoes (as dressy as you can without a war stamp). I would like some blue ones and white ones and tan ones. Bernard bought me three pair of red shoes in Montgomery. He just liked the way they were made. As it happened they were all red so he just bought them anyway. He is a mess.

I hope the money will help you some. I shall send you more when my allotment comes. Don't worry, I won't even miss a cent I sent you. We have more than enough. Bernard has made arrangements with the government to buy $150.00 worth of bonds a month. The government will take that out of his pay. I will get $100.00, his mother will get $50.00 and he will get to keep $100.00. So there will be plenty for all. (You see, he gets more money when he goes across seas.)

Well I've been to lunch and back again. I was in the officer's mess with Bernard. He just told me that they are leaving tomorrow night. I knew it for quite some time because I heard the conversation from the call from Washington. We are sworn to secrecy in our office so I couldn't tell even him. Gee everyone is leaving. I will write later.
Love Luana.

KIM

Later Luana writes:

LUANA

Hi Mom,

Once again I am writing you at work. I don't seem to get around to writing in the evenings. Usually when I get home, I fix dinner and hit the hay. With Bernard gone, I have nothing to do but go to bed.

The men left Friday night at midnight. There was a big party for the officer's that were leaving and their wives and sweethearts. The other officers bought cases and cases of beer for the fellows. They were all charged to the gills. Everybody was happy and gay until the last minute. Bernard and I sat on the front porch and talked until time for him to leave. He kept me laughing the whole evening. Now I know that he was doing it to keep us both from breaking down. He told me the things he was planning to do after the war. He said that we would probably have lots of arguments about money. I asked him why? He said he was going to make, or rather invest, in the motion picture business and I would probably disagree. He said it might even fail but even if it did, if I would stick by him, I would have nothing to worry about. He said while he was overseas, he was going to see about some of those countries. He said after the war, a man with a little money, can make a lot of money, in those war-torn countries. He said he would come back here and finish school, invest money in the picture business, and go back to Europe. These are his plans, whether they materialize or not only time will tell.

All the women broke down and cried and were hanging on to their husbands but not me. I kissed Bernard and he ran on down the steps yelling he would see me later. I watched him until I couldn't see him anymore. Everybody started calling me "Private", said I was the best soldier of the 99th.

I haven't heard from him yet but he promised to write before he left this country, if he could. They all had their packs on their backs, the officers carried pistols and beside all that, Bernard had to hand carry his typewriter, he would not leave it behind in case he had an idea for a story. He also had his steel helmet, plus camera. A guy gave him 100 feet of film so he can just snap away. He bought some developing fluid so he could develop his own pictures.

Well I'm going to stick it out here in Tuskegee until the last of May. Then I shall come home for a couple of weeks.

Luana

KIM

This took place in 1943. America faced two battlefields - war overseas, and riots here at home. Race riots erupted in Detroit, leaving more than thirty people dead. Sit-in demonstrations led by The Congress of Racial Equality began in a Chicago restaurant and spread across the country, as hundreds of Black Americans stood and protested the exclusion from civilian defense jobs. In the war overseas members of the 99th are in North Africa fighting in the air. Letter from Bernard to his bride:

BERNARD

Hello my darling Mrs. Knighten…this typewriter doesn't type worth two cents so ignore all mistakes…I find the beaches in North Africa much nicer than those in Europe…this is no hearsay but a result of personal observation…my dear…these mountains in Sicily are the thing…white…full of caves and very picturesque…and to see the people who have carved homes out of solid rocks in these mountains or built homes extending out over the edge of the mountain…I'm lost as I don't know a word of Italian…however lots of the Sicilians are formerly from the USA and they talk perfect English…I took a short hop to Africa the other day -- just a little business -- in other words I'm flying between continents…have gotten over that small time flying…This place is quite similar to North Africa but the people are different but just as poor…this war has really raised hell with the peoples in these parts…all of us are well…After flying twice today…I'm suddenly scheduled to fly again…well, great men are always misunderstood…hope this finds you as sweet as ever…yours truly misses you very much or do you know it…speculation has now begun as to the day we'll return to the states…but I still contend it's Christmas…am sleeping on the ground…my cot broke down and it's darn near impossible to think of getting another and impossible to get one, if I did think of getting one…The plane I named ol Lou, is running o.k. at this writing…but I've got my fingers crossed for anything with that name is bound to be dangerous…I ought to know…one object by that name ran into a guy one day, bowled him over like a tornado, and the dope hasn't been able to see straight yet….Here I am with about twenty bucks in French money and it's not worth a darn over here…but neither are you…I mean nether am I…so I think I'll just have to go to Paris to spend this money…---my new home has only a few lizards in it---oh well --- hello to everyone---don't know what's to become of us but I'm waiting to see---tons of love, forever yours, Bernard.

KIM

More from Bernard:

BERNARD

My Darling Lou…are you alright---I hope so, honey you probably know how I feel when I say fellow pilots White and McCullin are missing---yesterday was my day off and as expected I had a rotten time -- then to go out this morning and return to find they haven't landed--- now they're four hours overdue---we are expecting big shots this evening so I've got to shine these dusty shoes---better still I'll go to the beach, and lie in the sun maybe I'll feel better---darnit, I didn't write you yesterday, but perhaps you'll forgive me that only means I love you twice as much---I don't know maybe that's impossible---I think now if I loved you any more I'd probably burst---my bed is quite uncomfortable and I can't sleep---thus I dream of you all night long---I don't know whether it's good or bad---I miss the sleep but thinking of you is better than whisky or vitamin pills---hmmm---I'd better change that to just vitamin pills---the flies have taken over my domicile---another guy was burned by trying to pour gas on a flame--- these ducks will never learn---looks like the big shots are here---there's a transport overhead---I got money for mother's rental allowance before we were married-- -I put it in a bond and sent it to her---How is the Knighten finance's coming along---have you gotten any bond receipts as yet---are you buying bonds---tons of love---always, Bernard

KIM

Mail delivery during these years was erratic, never on time, and delays of weeks, even months were commonplace. Letters arrived out of sequence as in the example of this next letter:

LUANA

Hello Sweetheart,

Just went out in the streets to deposit some mail when I saw in big red letters "99th Pilot Killed". It scared me silly. I was afraid to walk over and buy the paper. I'm so nervous I can hardly write. Is this true? I'm losing confidence. Oh not in you, I don't doubt in the least that you are an ace flyer but I am scared stiff. Oh, if I could only see you, just get a glimpse of you or hear your voice. If I only had you here to let me lay my head on your shoulder and cry my eyeballs out and hear you tell me that everything is going to be o.k. then I would feel so much better. But I guess if you were here then I wouldn't have any need for tears. You do know that I love you so very much. I feel like an arm or some other vital part of my body is missing. You are my support and I can't go on without you. I don't get low in spirits often darling but for the past week it has been very tough. I promised myself that I would always write you cheerful letters and try not to let you know how much I miss you and how much a part of me you are. Oh, I better stop. I love you. I love you, so please, please be careful and come back to me.

Yours, Lou

KIM

Mail, telephone calls, and telegrams can bring terrifying news:

LUANA

Good Morning Darling,

Well I got a call from Montgomery just a few minutes ago. It was Mrs. White (White's Mother). She had read the papers and saw that I worked out here and that was how she knew where to call me. She told me she had received a letter yesterday from the War Department saying White had been missing since 2 July. I didn't know just what to say to her but after I had talked with her awhile, and I knew that she had control of herself, I told her just the things you had told me. I think I made her feel a little better and filled her full of hopes. She was even laughing when I hung up. She was so sad and on top of all that White's brother had just written her and said he was going overseas soon – and if that isn't enough ---- her daughter is in the WAC's (it is no longer the WAAC - the Army has taken things over and it is Women's Army Corps). I am going to write her after I finish this. I told her I would go to see her Sunday. I can catch that early train and leave in the afternoon. I shall send her address to yours and my Moms and they can write her and maybe she will feel better. It must be an awful shock to receive a brief telegram telling the one person you love most is gone and that you will never see them again. Please honey, see that I won't get one of those telegrams.

Lu

KIM

Fortunately, Luana did not receive one of those telegrams. Bernard, ever the humorist, did his best to keep his letters lighthearted. Sometimes he had help. December 27, 1943 – a letter to his mother-in-law:

BERNARD

Dearest Mom:

Received a funny note from a college chum. It was typed on toilet paper. He appears to think my last letter to him was bull-blankety blank. He felt compelled to answer my letter on stationary that "would be beneficial to you in days to come for I am certain you have run out of this choice paper." Sorry if this is a delicate matter, but you have to understand the friends I have attracted are not always delicate. Your gift and letter are an entirely different matter.

Santa Claus brought me your package and I'm truly grateful for this stationery. Pencils are almost unheard of in this sector - thanks so very much. Christmas was just another day so I had to invent the Christmas spirit. We were served turkey, with all the trimming - then the officer's bar had its grand opening with real American liquor. This didn't affect me, for I retired immediately after the dinner with a championship attack of indigestion probably from over-eating. Had plenty of company as my tent mate ate more than I, and had a worse case of the illness. So we went to bed groaning "silent night". My roommate is now out somewhere drinking. He found out today that he was the father of a seven-pound girl, so I don't know whether he's celebrating or trying to forget it. I suspect the latter for he wanted a boy.

Hope this finds you very happy following the Christmas season. Would really like to spend next Christmas in America. Hoping now, so I'll have 365 days for this dream to come true.

I received that truly glamorous photo of your eldest daughter. Had to look for some time to ascertain that this was the hen, I married. Finally decided that since Jean Harlow was dead, this was Luana, the girl I married.

There is a strong wind in this valley from across the nearby snow-capped mountains; And this valley must be much colder than even the mountains. I'm sitting almost atop the stove, which gives off more smoke than heat. It seems as if any moment this flimsy tent will collapse. If it does, I'll not move, much to cold to bother about fixing a tent tonight. Tons of love, your son-in-law, Bernard.

KIM

Letter to Luana's Mother from Bernard:

BERNARD

Dear Mom,

I hope this finds you and the family as fine as your handsome son. Except for a few minor ails, everything is all right in North Africa. I named my airplane after your beautiful daughter Luana, and it hasn't run right since. I suppose the three other brats are fine now that school is out, too bad they can't splash around in the Mediterranean Sea with us all day … as we have no bathtubs, we swim and bathe in one stroke. I had an abandoned German jeep until yesterday. We put an aero plane battery in it and the darn thing had too much power … the result … our jeep burned up. The Red Cross sent doughnuts for the officers and men. When they arrived, the officers were up flying and didn't get a taste. I'm sick over it because for a whole week, I dreamt about those doughnuts. Here the natives or Arabs make the women do all the work. The men ride the donkeys while his wife walks behind him, bent all over under a load of hay or something. It's really a shame how they work the women. We have been here for two months now and all are still O.K. The men have hurt each other with German rifles and motorcycles but that's all. French and Arabic are the languages here and we all mess up the little we know. So even the natives don't understand. I've learned to boil and wash clothes better than a laundry … if you daughter can iron, we'll go into business after the war. Again, hello to all the family.

Yours, Bernard

KIM

January 12, 1944, Luana has left Alabama and moved to the big city. From the office of L&T Certified Public Accountants, West 125th St. NY – From Luana to Bernard:

LUANA

Hello Sweetheart,

Just saw a newspaper and at the bottom of the paper I saw where Spanky and Jamie were promoted…

Congrats to them. Relay my messages. Also read of your 46 sorties, congrats to you to my beautiful baby and please keep the good work up. And please hurry home.

Well I have decided to give up the idea of getting a place of my own. Neither of my play-Mothers agree and both say you won't either. Marie gave me a long lecture yesterday on the foolishness of buying even the first bit of furniture – even secondhand stuff when you might come home tomorrow. I told Effie I was thinking of moving so she cut my rent down to eight dollars a week. That includes meals too, of course. Guess I can't beat that. Sure hate to tell Harriet though, we had been haunting the second hand shops and real estate offices. But I guess the mothers know best, I just wanted something I could call my own. But I guess that is rather childish, maybe I still haven't grown up. I don't know. I guess I am just lost without you. Please be careful and come back to me.

Marie brought up some points that I can't help but mention. It scared the devil out of me as I never thought of it. She said, that you can't help but lose a little confidence in me and doubt me, because you are idle. And, that when you come back you will be changed. Not necessary your feelings towards me but in lots of other ways. Also, you have achieved fame and women are going to run after you. So many other things she mentioned that it really has me worried. I never thought of all those things. I don't believe you will hurt me, well, all I can do is keep my fingers crossed. Must go home…it is past six o'clock…I love you, yours always,

Luana

KIM

It is May 15, 1945 – Three weeks after German dictator Adolph Hitler committed suicide. One week after Germany surrendered and the military allowed white pilots with 60 points to leave the war theater and return to their home base. Here is Luana's letter from Fort Knox, Kentucky:

LUANA

Hi Mummy,

Well, here I am in Louisville or rather close to it. But I am afraid it won't be for long. Spratmo (you know, gossip) is flying thick and fast. Some say we won't be here but a few days…some say a couple of weeks… Some say, the group is going to a point of embarkation. Others say, we are going north to a field there. It is really a mess. The Army really makes a problem of these race officers. They just don't seem to know what to do with the colored pilots. Twenty of the returning pilots in Tuskegee had enough points and left Saturday for civilian life. Bernard has 87 points and went to the CO here and signed all the papers to get out of the army but I'm afraid it is all in vain. The CO argues colored officers are still needed. We would have a chance anywhere else, but not in this group. But I'm praying and hoping. It would really be wonderful to settle down to a normal life.

The Kentucky Derby is June 9th. I'm hoping like mad that we will be here for it. I wanted you to come down for it but with the situation as it is, I can't make any plans. Fort Knox is a huge place with plenty of segregation. They keep all the spooks in one area. Even their airplanes are segregated. It is really disgusting. It makes me boil to see how nice they treat the German prisoners on the field. Those guys are really living the life. I have noticed that the prisoners live next to the whites then the Negroes live in <u>back</u> of the prisoners. It really hurts Mom, and these guys <u>really</u> feel it. Lots of guys are getting court marshaled or anything to get out of this swindle. A few guys are trying to Uncle Tom their way through, and boy are they a mess. No one can stand them. Love Lu.

Essence 1946

KIM

Bernard left the active military life for being a reserve. He became the second Black air traffic controller in U.S. stationed at LaGuardia, New York. He and Luana created a hectic, happy life, steadily building toward their dreams. Here the military pilot turned civilian publisher talks about his latest business venture. New York 1946:

BERNARD

Dear Mom:

Luana and I published our first issue of <u>Essence Magazine</u>. With the aid of aspiring writers at the Harlem Writers Workshop we put it out. Luana hopes the money we spent doesn't put us out of house. I'll be sending you a copy next week. We got a talented young writer named Alex Haley to write for us, and those fancy New York designers gave us a mink or two. I'm still waiting for the sheriff to take us away. Here's something I wrote about our mission:

"It must be admitted that there is a need for some medium through which women of our race can be instructed in the art of properly purchasing and wearing clothes. It cannot be denied that the many fashion magazines on the stands today have absolutely nothing in common with the demands of the brown-skinned woman...to dress, and dress properly, in colors and designs that will give our women the best possible appearance is the object of this magazine."

Pretty high brow stuff! I wrote a poetic piece for Luana, but she takes offense to it. Mom, you tell me what you think:

It's called: Susie Plots goes dancing

> Sue gets an invite to a dance. She's off and on
>   the run.
> Buying hats, shoes, everything, It's Susie's
>   night for fun.
> From 12 to 2 she's' on the hop, She flits from
>   here to there;
> From 2 to 4 her glamour thrives, By settings in
>   her hair.
> From 4 to 7 she sleeps in peace, Beneath a film
>   of cream.
> And 7 to 8, she in the tub to give her skin that
>   gleam.
> From 9 to 12, she dresses with care, Just like
>   the queen of the ball;
> And half past twelve, she coolly strolls, Into the
>   crowded hall.
> Twelve hours she worked to look her best, To
>   make the tongues all wag;
> Yet when the dance has reached its end,
> My Susie looks like an old hag.

You think it's funny huh Mom? Don't you Mom?
Mom? Love Bernard.

KIM

Essence Magazine lasted through four fabulous issues, and
then flopped. However, Bernard's days as a civilian ended
when President Truman committed troops to Korea in
1950.   With Bernard flying again Luana pursued her
theatrical dream.   It is Friday, Aug 8, 1954, As Luana
would quote "Que sera, sera":

LUANA

Hi Mom,

I guess you've heard from Bernard by now. Yes he came home for one week, and the time went so fast, he was gone before I knew it. I hope he enjoyed his stay because I didn't. We didn't have one minute alone. So help me I am going to get a room somewhere. Well, not really, but our popularity is getting me down. We always have a house full of people…like Grand Hotel or something. Anyway, I was so glad to see my baby…he is as sweet as ever. Be glad when we can be together.

Now for my good fortune! As you know I have been playing around with different theater groups and at last I am going to be in a Broadway show. I am understudying three roles and I start rehearsal on Aug 15. We open in Philadelphia in September before we come into Broadway. I am really thrilled. Now I will be a member of Equity and will be able to get other jobs. The play is called *Take a Giant Step*. As you can see I am really going all out for this radio and theater business. I was given an audition for radio station WLIB here in NY and I feel that I will get an hour show on Saturday and possibly a disc jockey show during the week. If I get these shows plus the one on Broadway I will have it made. Hot dog! Maybe I'll get to buy that house for you yet. Told Bernard that within next year I plan to be making $500.00 a week. He says he believes I will too, and for me to hurry up and start making it so I can buy him a Cadillac. Oh, there is someone at the door. I'll write later tomorrow. Love Lu.

KIM

December 1954:

LUANA

Mummy: Merry Christmas, and here's the news.   I'm pregnant! I'll write later. Lu

LUANA EXITS

KIM

I was born in July. When Luana returned to work, after my birth, she won a leading role in the play Take a Giant Step. *Among its stars was a 16 year old named Lou Gossett Jr. It was to open September 25, 1956.*

Two days before opening night, a baby-sitter arrived at the house to take care of me, but found Luana laying on the living room floor, beside the vacuum cleaner. Luana lay dead before her. The medical report reads heart failure. Luana was buried at Evergreen Cemetery, Brooklyn, New York, September 27, 1956. In this final letter, Bernard writes about life without his calendar girl. Friday night.

BERNARD

Dear Mom:

Started ten letters and never finished one. Hope you and Dad are fine. Kim and I are okay. I saw Kim last night and she's the greatest thing alive. Not talking any sense yet, but will talk anyway. Maybe somebody, someplace can understand that jabbering, but her poor father can't understand a word his daughter is saying. Honest Mom she is so fine. Am mad now that Luana and I didn't have a dozen kids.

They had the bank account tied up until last week. Seems as if anytime there is more than 400 dollars, they have to get a release, and with the safe deposit box, they had to look for a will. Nothing found, so now the money is free and I can pay those funeral bills. I'm putting the house up for sale, everyone tells me I can get ten to twelve thousand for it. I'll buy a building in Manhattan if that is correct. I'm so easy with money its a wonder Luana and I have anything, the way we threw money away. But I think it paid off. Looks like the more we gave away, the more we got, so I don't think I'll ever be able to change now. Maybe Kim will have some money sense. She'd better have some sense or I'll shoot her.

I'm putting the scrapbook in order slowly. Will have to buy a bigger safe deposit box now for I want to keep this in a safe place for Kim to know about later.

Sister left the next night after you did but after a big struggle. The plane was to leave at 1:00 a.m. At 11 p.m., Brother Claiborne took Kim home and all of Kim's clothing. He also mistakenly took Sister's luggage.

Then he had to meet me at the bridge and I sped like mad to meet him. Naturally, the cops stopped me for speeding and after hearing my tale let me go on speeding. We made it with ten minutes to spare.
All else is well except I miss my calendar girl Luana. Maybe one of these days I'll be able to write a novel or story about her. I have to fly early in the morning, love to you.

Your son, Bernard

BERNARD EXITS

KIM OPENS A BOX OF LETTERHEAD AND BEGINS WRITING A LETTER

KIM

Dear Luana,

[*Kim pauses and repeatedly struggles to find the right phrase*],

Dear Mommy? Mother? Mom,

This is awkward. I don't know how to address you.

I wish you could see me and I would know it somehow because I want to thank you for the beautiful collection of letters you and Dad wrote and saved. The full collection of 400 plus letters is the most valuable treasure I own.

I wish I could talk to you. I'd start by telling you I'm fine. Dad provided for me in every way he knew how. We both know he wasn't perfect. He was flawed, and loving and gentle and maddening as anyone. Yet he did his best to see I had whatever a little girl needed – food, water, a roof over my head, college tuition.

Aunt Peaches and Uncle Clay took me in and tried to spoil me. Piano lessons, dance lessons, ughh...dressing me up like a little doll for photos. Me: with my white patent leather shoes, white ruffled socks, petite little skirt dress, white gloves, bangs and two perfectly balanced braids. I lived in that loving home filled with wonderful older, protective, older [she says it humorously] brothers and a boxer dog named Brownie. Sounds idyllic, doesn't it? Did I mention it was in the Bronx?

Yet and still it was very much Ozzie and Harriet, meets Leave it to Beaver, and The Cosby's and Tupac. [Kim laughs] I'm sorry, you may not know these people. They are television comedy series characters and a rapper. What's a rapper? [Kim demonstrates a rap quip] And you know television, but you may not know that television went from being black and white in the living room to being full color in every room, every car and on every phone. Oh yeah and phones – they are cellular – umm, portable. We carry them on our person – no wires either. Everyone has a personal phone number, like a social security number. Is social security still around? Let me get back to you on that? I wish I could hear your voice. I'd understand why Grandma always said I had your voice. Would the infant inside of me recognize the sound, the pitch, the love?

I wish I could touch you, maybe I could grieve. I was an infant at your death leaving no memories of you.

To lose a parent before memories are formed is either a tragedy or a blessing – I can't say which.

                         [*Anger begins to grow in Kim*]
I wish I could understand why Dad never spoke about you. He lived to be almost 80. During his lifetime, he never shared stories, never referred to you. Never said I looked like you, except when prompted by your sisters. Whatever his reason he couldn't or wouldn't communicate anything about you to me.

         [*Surprise and understanding replace anger in Kim*]
And yet, he left this treasure of letters for me. Did I sound angry? I don't feel that way. Once I did, but drugs and therapy solved that.

Dad and me, we went on with our lives and he blessed me with a larger family filled with evolving challenges and wonderful gifts of love. I loved Dad immensely and we grew close in his later years. He turned out to be a wonderful father.

No, I don't have a right to be angry. I do have the responsibility to acknowledge my father was a single parent and I understand my having only one parent, especially a caring parent is a blessing.

There are many children without parents or loving families going through life's struggles alone. So if you were here, I would ask you to pray with me for the children who have lost parents prematurely. We would pray for the widowed parent struggling without support and without direction, trying to raise their children.

We would pray that every parent would create a legacy of letters – a Bernard and Luana tribute - for their children to discover and explore.

So I send these thoughts to you Luana – My Mother. Love, your daughter,

Kim

Lights out   THE END

Meet Kim Knighten Russell

I am...the daughter of Luana and Bernard Knighten.

Professionally I am…an experienced arts administrator, performance artist and more…

My work has been focused in two areas: 1) in arts administration as a director for a regional nonprofit; 2) dedicated to arts integration as the education coordinator for a performing arts center. The range of these experiences include managing teams of artists; Developing and delivering arts education programming; Service on state-wide and national commissions; Grant writing and review panel experience; Contract negotiations with touring arts performances, and community and coalition building. With over 16 years in the arts, as an administrator, writer and performer, combined with a Master's Degree in business, I am confident in my abilities.

I am an experienced touring artist…
I have performed at colleges and library conferences in my one-woman show on the life of Sojourner Truth, since 1996. My performances have taken me coast-to-coast with an invitation to perform in South Africa followed by a visit to The White House. I perform as a humanities scholar in Chautauqua fashion and as a solo artist in my original comedy "Life After 50: Survivalist Training Required".

I am a playwright…
I possess more than 400 letters written during World War II and I have developed a one-act play called "The Tuskegee Love Letters". The letters have become the basis of the 13-episode television series registered with the Writer's Guild West called "Harlem", written by Byron Tidwell and Kim Russell. A book full of more letters, expanding this story is due out in 2013.

I am a consultant and mentor…
I serve as an advisor to numerous performing arts organizations. I read and review grant submissions. I mentor novice solo performers.

I am...grateful.
December 12, 2011

Meet Jay Bernard
Watch Jay's comic debut on BET ComicView at:

www.jaybernardcomedy.com

Host a reading
of *Tuskegee Love Letters* in your community.
                              Contact kimrussell@earthlink.net

Coming Soon:

The complete story of Luana's journey from how she met Bernard, to her travels in the U.S and abroad, to her movie career, prior to her stage career.

Coming Soon:

HARLEM cable series
Inspired by letters written by Bernard
and Luana Knighten
Adapted by BYRON TIDWELL
© 2008 Kim K. Russell and Byron Tidwell

Learn more about the television series based on the prolific writings of the founder of a magazine called Essence 1946. The series tells the dramatic story of the Harlem community from World War II through the beginnings of the Civil Rights Era. Harlem is at once a love story, a story of patriotism, a story of the fight against racism, and a story of transcendence and accomplishment. The hidden history of the vibrant Harlem community comes to light in this touching, personal series

Kim Russell
3395 S Jones 206
Las Vegas, Nevada 89146-6729
kimrussell@earthlink.net

Kim Russell as
Sojourner Truth

An American Hero
An Abolitionist
An Advocate for Women's Rights

Award winning Chautauqua, Humanities Scholar

Made in the USA
Lexington, KY
06 October 2012